I0845843

Dealing with Multi-Factor Authentication (MFA) Issues

Table of Contents

Chapter 1. Introduction

In today's increasingly digital and interconnected world, securing our data and online identities has never been more vital. Our Special Report aims to shed light on a crucial piece of this security puzzle - Multi-Factor Authentication (MFA). Whilst MFA is a widely recommended security measure, it comes with its own set of challenges that organizations and individuals need to effectively navigate. This report is meticulously designed to offer you an accessible, down-to-earth analysis of these MFA challenges, ensuring that the complexities of the subject matter don't impede your understanding. By revealing real-world case studies, expert insights, and practical mitigation strategies, our Special Report offers an essential, comprehensive guide to resolving MFA issues - a grapple you no longer need to face alone.

Chapter 2. Understanding the Basics of Multi-Factor Authentication

Multi-Factor Authentication (MFA) is not just another buzzword in the cybersecurity world. It is a significant step towards stronger data protection, especially in this era characterized by digitalization, interconnectivity, and advances in hacking methodologies.

MFA involves the use of two or more different types of validation methods in an authentication mechanism. To understand this better, let's initially dive into what makes MFA a worthwhile security measure.

2.1. Why MFA Matters

For most digital systems, the standard security protocol is simply entering a username and a password - something you know. However, passwords alone have long proved to be vulnerable to breach attempts. MFA tackles this vulnerability by adding another layer(s) of defense. If one security factor is breached, an attacker would still have to get past the second or possibly even a third.

2.2. Components of MFA

There are generally three accepted categories of MFA credentials: 1. Something you know (knowledge): This is usually a password, a PIN, or answers to security questions. 2. Something you have (possession): This often refers to a physical device, such as a secure token or a smartphone, used to confirm one's identity. 3. Something you are (inherence): This involves biometrics - unique characteristics like fingerprints, facial patterns, IRIS patterns, voice, or behavior.

A robust MFA system requires at least two of the above credential types, retrieved via separate channels, to authenticate a user.

2.3. Working of MFA

To understand the intricacies of MFA's operation, consider a banking app for example. When logging in, aside from entering a password (something you know), you might also be required to enter a code sent to your phone (something you have) or validate your fingerprint (something you are). Each step is a separate authentication factor, together constituting MFA.

2.4. Types of MFA

There are various MFA methods, categorizable based on the type of credential used and the need for physical hardware:

1. Hardware Tokens: Businesses traditionally used hardware tokens, which generate one-time passwords (OTPs). However, they are costly and can be stolen or lost.

2. Software Tokens: These are applications that generate OTPs, minimizing the need for carrying a separate device.

3. SMS and Email: These methods utilize a message or email (with an OTP or link) sent to a user's device.

4. Biometric: Biometrics is emerging as a popular MFA method due to its uniqueness to each individual.

Remember that the effectiveness of MFA usually greatly depends on the execution of these layers.

2.5. Challenges with MFA

While MFA significantly increases security, it is not without its challenges:

1. User Experience: As MFA procedures increase, the potential friction for users also enhances. The key is to find a balance between security and ease-of-use.

2. Cost Factor: Implementing MFA can be expensive, particularly for larger corporations with a significant user base.

3. Managing Lost Possession Factors: Lost or stolen hardware or personnel changes can cause issues.

While these challenges might make MFA seem intimidating, they are manageable. It's about weighing the relative risks and rewards and implementing solutions that keep your data secure while also being user-friendly.

2.6. Mitigating MFA Challenges

To regulate these problems, various solutions can be adapted:

1. Adaptive MFA: It adjusts to the behavior of the user, determining when to ask for further authentication to improve user experience.

2. Cost-effective Solutions: Opting for software tokens instead of hardware or utilizing biometric capabilities on users' phones can be cost-effective methods.

3. Clear Policies: Drafting and disseminating clear policies for lost devices and changes in personnel can also help to mitigate issues.

In summary, while MFA isn't immune to issues, it's one of the most robust mechanisms available to protect data. It's essential to approach its implementation strategically, considering both the unique benefits and challenges it brings. Armed with this fundamental understanding, we can examine more advanced topics, like MFA's application and management techniques, in the following sections.

Chapter 3. The Power and Importance of Multi-Factor Authentication

In an increasingly digital sphere, one principle rings true above all others - "Never depend on a single point of failure." And so, we come to understand the immense power of Multi-Factor Authentication (MFA), a boon to those who aspire to create a secure online landscape.

MFA inherently operates under the mantle of robustness that it creates by having multiple layers of security gates. Imagine a castle, but instead of one drawbridge and moat ring, you have multiple of these circumventing the fortress. Each ring of protection is a unique form of authentication a user must pass through to authenticate their identity.

3.1. The Principle of MFA

Let's first explore how MFA functions. It leans on the aspect of a person knowing something (knowledge), having something (possession), or being someone (inherence). These three factors form MFA's pillars. An optimal MFA strategy could involve a complex intertwining of these factors, providing well-rounded security.

1. Knowledge-based authentication utilizes information that only the user should know, such as a password or a PIN.

2. Possession-based authentication relies on something physical the user should have - a smart card, security token, or even a mobile device receiving a one-time passcode (OTP).

3. Inherence-based authentication is grounded in the unique biological characteristics of the user, i.e., biometrics such as

fingerprints, facial patterns, or voice recognition.

3.2. MFA in Action: A Real-World Paradigm

In a real-world context, consider banking. Typically, to access your online account, you enter your username (something you know). This first layer of authentication is not immensely secure, considering that it can be lost or stolen.

The second layer could be an OTP sent to your mobile device (something you possess). Now, the stakes are higher for a potential attacker since they must have access to your phone or the ability to intercept the OTP.

Biometrics forms the last bulwark. For instance, using facial recognition (something inherent to you) ensures that even if an attacker bypasses the first two layers, they must mimic your facial features - a challenging task with modern facial recognition technology.

3.3. Advantages of MFA

At its core, MFA is about exponentially increasing the difficulty for an attacker to gain unauthorized access. This amplification of security is the primary benefit of MFA, but it extends beyond this point.

1. Risk-based approach: MFA can dynamically adjust the authentication requirements based on the perceived risk, taking into account several variables like location, time, and behavior patterns.

2. Compliance: Data protection regulations increasingly mandate the use of MFA, thereby assisting businesses in their compliance journey.

3. User convenience: From an end-user perspective, biometric authentication methods are typically quicker and easier to use than traditional passwords.

However, while MFA is a mighty fortress, it's essential to know that like any castle, it's not invincible.

3.4. Challenges in MFA

Despite its tenacity, MFA isn't without its drawbacks. Complex implementations can confuse users and lead to reduced productivity. Moreover, certain factors of MFA, if compromised, can potentially lead to breaches. It's also worth noting that MFA deployment could potentially be a costly affair for businesses, both in terms of finance and time.

3.5. Overcoming Challenges: To Fortify Your Castle

So how do we tackle these challenges? Primarily, it's about striking a balance. User-friendliness must be married to robust security. While robust, MFA should not hamper the user experience substantially - it's a balancing act.

1. Risk-based MFA: This model provides an excellent starting point. The system evaluates the level of risk associated with a user or transaction and then applies the appropriate level of security.

2. Continuous monitoring and validation: The security landscape is not static, and neither should an MFA system be. Regularly validate the security measures in place and evolve them as threats evolve.

3. Educating Users: Users need to understand why MFA matters, how it works, and what their role is in maintaining security. Awareness and training are two significant aspects of making

MFA work effectively.

Overall, MFA provides a stellar fortification but like any castle, it requires regular maintenance and strategic planning to ensure its strength stays undiminished. Balancing the nuanced aspects of implementation and user convenience with the hardness of the security system will ensure that MFA is wielded as the mighty tool it should be.

Chapter 4. Common Issues Encountered with Multi-Factor Authentication

User Misperception and Education ===

One of the most common issues encountered with MFA is the prevalent misperception among users about its functionality, and in large part, this springs from a lack of proper education. Many users (both within organizations and outside) view MFA as an unnecessary and complicated step to accessing their accounts.

Users often perceive MFA as an inconvenience that stretches out the usual login process. For instance, they may feel frustrated at needing additional authentication components – something they know (password), something they have (smartphone), or something they are (biometrics) – beyond the traditional fixed password.

To address this issue, better education on the importance and functionality of MFA should be prioritized. Users need to understand that MFA provides a triple layer of protection which means that even if one factor is compromised, the attacker would still need to bypass the others making it exponentially harder to gain illegitimate access.

Practically, this could be done through regular training programs, user-friendly tutorials, or even integrating interactive demonstrations during the MFA setup process.

Technical Difficulties and Incompatibility ===

Technical issues represent another significant challenge with MFA. For instance, the user might face difficulties in receiving authentication codes due to poor network coverage or issues with their mobile service provider. Even the intricate process of setting up

MFA might dissuade some users due to technical incompatibilities or implementation issues.

Certain MFA methods might also be incompatible with older device models or certain operating systems. This problem could be especially prevalent in organizational settings where a diverse array of devices can be used, all with varying levels of compatibility with different MFA mechanisms.

Organizations need to ensure available technical support for ongoing issues. Further, selecting MFA solutions with wide compatibility (across different device types, operating models, operating systems) should be prioritized. Companies should also consider flexibility in their MFA approach – such as providing a variety of authentication methods to cater to this diverse device ecosystem.

Lost or Misplaced Authentication Factor ===

In cases where the authentication factor is a physical device such as a phone or token, there might be instances where the user could lose or misplace the item. In such scenarios, the user would be unable to authenticate and access their account, leading to potential productivity loss or even data risk if the access token falls into the wrong hands.

One way to mitigate this risk is by implementing backup authentication methods. By giving users the ability to link multiple devices or have options like security questions, organizations can ensure that even if one authentication factor is lost, business operations will not be hindered.

Users Forgetting Security Information ===

For MFA methods that involve 'something you know,' such as passwords or answers to security questions, there's a risk that users might forget their information. This becomes especially true as best practices encourage complex and non-repetitive passwords or answers.

Techniques like implementing password managers can help users remember their credentials without compromising on complexity. Also, the use of biometric data can eliminate the need to remember complex passwords entirely by relying on 'something you are.'

Privacy Concerns Around Biometrics ===

With advancements in technology, biometric authentication methods such as fingerprints and facial recognition are becoming more prevalent. However, these also raise significant privacy concerns. Users might feel uncomfortable sharing their biometric data due to the fear of potential misuse – given it's data that can't be changed, unlike a password.

To address this issue, organizations need to ensure they have solid data privacy and security measures in place. Clear communication about how biometric data is stored, used, and protected can alleviate user concerns. The promise of ensuring encryption and not sharing such data with third parties will foster trust and increase user acceptance.

Final Thoughts ===

Despite these challenges, it's essential to emphasize that the benefits of MFA significantly outweigh the drawbacks. Though issues like user misperception, technical difficulties, lost authentication factors, forgotten security information, and privacy concerns pose legitimate problems, they can be successfully mitigated with the right measures. All organizations, large and small, should be on the frontline, championing the adoption of MFA, as it is a robust front in the battle against cyber threats.

Chapter 5. Anatomy of a Successful MFA Implementation

Durability, scalability, and security arc the three cornerstones that form the bedrock of any successful Multi-Factor Authentication (MFA) implementation. However, to forge these elements into a relentless safeguard for your digital realm, it's essential to understand their inner workings, intertwined relationships, and the delicate art of their orchestration.

5.1. The Durability of MFA

Durability defines the MFA's ability to stand the test of time and adapt to continuously evolving cyber threats. Durability requires a robust recovery system and flexibility for additions or changes in security policies. Balance is key here: an excessively rigid system struggles to adapt, while an overly flexible one becomes prone to human error.

A reliable MFA recovery system is crucial, providing users with alternative methods of access in case primary factors become ineffective. This could involve incorporating biometric data, security questions, secondary email addresses, or backup codes. Regularly prompting users to update recoverability information is a must, keeping the system updated and user accounts secure.

Moreover, MFA solutions should allow security policy adjustments with relative ease. This provides the ability to incorporate new or upgraded authentication factors as they become available. For example, replacing less secure SMS verification with token-based authentication. However, security teams must take care not to transition too hastily, as abrupt policy changes might prompt user resistance.

5.2. The Scalability of MFA

Scalability pertains to the MFA solution's ability to cater to an expanding user base, both quantitatively and geographically. An MFA solution should have the capacity to handle growing numbers of users and increasingly complex infrastructures. It should not only adapt to corporate growth but also stay ahead of the curve when it comes to expected expansions.

Scalability involves the implementation of an effective identity management system that streamlines user onboarding, offboarding, and role modification processes. It must seamlessly integrate with an organization's existing software systems, reducing redundancy and ensuring uninterrupted operation.

Geographically diverse users add another layer of complexity. An effective MFA solution must remain inclusive, accommodating different users' specific needs and capabilities. It should meet regional data protection requirements and manage internet connectivity issues that may arise due to geographical distribution.

5.3. The Security of MFA

Security, the third cornerstone, goes beyond the incorporation of multiple authentication factors. It involves continuous monitoring and threat detection, user education and awareness, and a well-defined incident response plan.

Continuous monitoring identifies suspicious behavior in real time, triggering immediate actions. Unusual login locations or repeated login failures might suggest a potential attack, necessitating swift response.

User education is just as significant. Users must understand why MFA is necessary, how it works, and what they can do to reinforce its effectiveness. This includes understanding the dangers of weak passwords, threats from phishing emails, and the importance of keeping personal devices secure.

Having an incident response plan in place is key. Despite all preventive measures, security breaches can occur, at which point, damage control and swift remedial measures become paramount.

5.4. Assembling The Cornerstones: Implementation Strategy

Developing an effective MFA implementation strategy involves five primary stages: Assessment, Planning, Execution, Testing, and Evaluation.

Assessment involves a comprehensive analysis of the organization's needs, available resources, and potential vulnerabilities.

Planning succeeds assessment, outlining a detailed roadmap, establishing communication channels, arranging resource allocation, and drafting contingency plans.

Execution follows the roadmap meticulously, ensuring each milestone is achieved within the set timelines. Regular reviews and adjustments are necessary for the course of action to stay aligned with its objectives.

Testing involves rigorous validation and bug fixing. This process can be both time-consuming and redundant; however, it's crucial for robust error-proof functionality of the MFA system.

Evaluation, the final step, assesses the system after it has been functioning for some time. This step ensures that the system is capable of withstanding real-world scenarios and caters effectively to the organization's needs.

In summary, a successful MFA implementation requires a meticulous strategy, a comprehensive understanding of the organization's needs, and a clear vision of its digital landscape. While challenges are inevitable, the durability, scalability, and security that a well-implemented MFA solution provides far outweigh the initial complexities.

Chapter 6. Dealing with User Resistance to MFA

Resistance to change is an age-old issue that all organizations and systems face, especially when implementing new technologies like Multi-Factor Authentication (MFA). No matter how beneficial a change might be, there is often resistance due to various factors, including lack of awareness, confusion or fear of the new procedure, and concern about potential disruptions to already established workflows.

6.1. Understanding User Resistance

Understanding the reasons behind user resistance is the first step in dealing with it. The nature of resistance can range from active opposition to passive non-compliance. Some common reasons for resistance towards MFA include:

- Perception that MFA complicates the login procedure

- Privacy concerns

- Insufficient communication about the benefits and necessity of MFA

- Low risk perception – "it won't happen to me"

- Fear of change and new technology

Each of these points can be addressed to gradually eliminate resistance, but patience and consistent communication are key.

6.2. Overcoming the Perception of Complexity

One of the major pushbacks against MFA is the belief that it adds unnecessary complexity to the login procedure. While it's true that MFA does add an extra layer of security checks during login, this additional step is designed to safeguard the user's data.

To address this concern, organizations need to communicate the risk of data breaches and the potential havoc they can wreak on personal and professional life. Defining and sharing case studies of security breaches can be an effective method of demonstrating the severity of such incidences.

Moreover, introducing users to user-friendly MFA methods can reduce the perception of complexity. For instance, biometric authentication (fingerprint or facial recognition) and push notifications are often seen as less intrusive and easier to handle than, say, a randomly generated code sent via email or text message.

6.3. Addressing Privacy Concerns

Privacy concerns are always paramount when discussing online security. Many users are troubled by the idea of sharing personal data, like a phone number, which is commonly required for MFA methods like SMS codes.

To address these concerns, organizations should:

- Ensure their privacy policies are up-to-date, comprehensive, and transparent.

- Clarify what information is needed for MFA, why it's needed, and how it will be used and protected.

- Explore MFA methods that require minimal personal

information.

Privacy concerns can be more persistent and may require continued reassurance and open lines of communication.

6.4. Increasing Risk Perception

There's a common belief among many users that they are not likely to be targets of cyberattacks. This tends to lower their perceived need for high-security measures, such as the ones MFA provides.

To increase risk perception, organizations can:

- Share statistics and real-life examples of small-scale, individual hackers as well as large-scale data breaches.

- Conduct regular security awareness training.

- Use phishing simulation tests to demonstrate how easily anyone could fall for a seemingly harmless email or message.

This needs to be done in a non-threatening manner to avoid creating a climate of fear or paranoia.

6.5. Gently Transitioning to New Technologies

Change, particularly surrounding technology, can be daunting for many people. Consequently, organizations should introduce MFA in stages. A potential strategy could be:

- Preliminary announcements and educational campaigns about the upcoming change.

- Transition periods where MFA is optional.

- Regular check-ins and support sessions to help users through their transition.

- Gradual enforcement of MFA, perhaps initially just for more sensitive procedures.

This gradual and supportive approach can help assuage fears and encourage more users to get onboard.

6.6. Conclusion

Resistance to MFA is a challenge that can be overcome with adequate planning, communication, and training. Understanding the reasons behind the resistance allows for tailored approaches that address user concerns, enhance risk perception, and simplify the transition to new technologies. By doing so, organizations not only heighten their security but also encourage a more security-conscious culture amongst their users.

Chapter 7. Case Study: Resolving MFA Challenges in Business Settings

One of the key aspects of dealing with Multi-Factor Authentication (MFA) concerns is understanding how these challenges manifest in real-world scenarios. This chapter presents a case study focused on the multifaceted issues faced by businesses and how businesses can approach the resolution of these instances.

7.1. The Company Profile

Our case study revolves around a mid-sized e-commerce company providing a variety of services online, ranging from online retail to subscription-based services. Given the diverse range of services provided, and the interplay between their users and their system, they adopted MFA to ensure security, especially because of the sensitive customer data contained within their systems.

7.2. Pre-MFA Scenario

Their initial security measures solely consisted of the traditional username and password verification method. Over a period of time, as instances of unauthorized access and data breaches increased, the company felt the need to up the ante on their security systems. This consideration, complemented by the globally increasing dominance and subsequent recommendation for MFA, led them to implement it into their security solutions.

7.3. Challenges Post MFA Implementation

After the adoption of MFA, a myriad of challenges began to manifest. The three prongs of these challenges encompassed customer satisfaction, technological glitches, and administrative issues.

7.3.1. Technological Glitches

The company used biometric scans in combination with a password as a form of MFA. Some users with older devices weren't able to access their services as their devices didn't support the updated MFA system. Critical software patches were also missed, which led to security vulnerabilities.

7.3.2. Customer Dissatisfaction

Many customers found the addition of biometric scanning as a cumbersome step, leading to a lot of dissatisfaction and a sizable drop-off rate. Some users also found it difficult to navigate and understand, which again caused frustration and drop-offs.

7.3.3. Administrative Concerns

The adoption of MFA also brought a number of administrative issues. These involved higher costs because of software procurement and implementation, increased need for tech support, and conducting employee training sessions to properly handle the new security measure.

7.4. Resolving MFA Challenges

The resolution of the MFA challenges was administered by recognizing the pressing issues and addressing them systematically.

7.4.1. Overcoming Technological Hurdles

Software patches were immediately initiated to close security loopholes. For users with older device models, the option was provided to use SMS or email verification as the second factor authentication in lieu of biometric verification. This ensured that user experience didn't suffer due to older technology.

7.4.2. Addressing User Experience Issues

A major overhaul of the user experience was undertaken. The MFA process was made more intuitive and less time-consuming. A proper user onboarding campaign was launched that entailed emails, on-site pop-ups, and educational videos explaining the process of MFA to users.

7.4.3. Tackling Administrative Problems

On the administrative end, cost-benefit analysis showed that the security benefits far outweighed the initial setup costs. Steps were also taken to streamline tech support and, instead of treating MFA as a separate entity, it was woven into the fabric of regular operations so employee training could be minimal and seamless.

7.5. Final Thoughts

The challenges of implementing MFA are indeed of various origin and not trivial. However, with careful planning and proactive customer communication, they can be mitigated. The case study of our e-commerce venture shows that despite hitting initial turbulence, they managed to successfully implement MFA without compromising customer happiness or their bottom line.

Adopting a multi-factor authentication system is not a one-size-fits-all solution. Many factors like the nature of the business, the technological adeptness of its user base, and in-house capabilities need to be considered before tailoring an MFA solution that fits best. It is a balancing act between ensuring rock-solid security and providing seamless user experience. But as challenging as it may be, in today's digital world, it's a mandatory investment that reaps its rewards in securing a company's digital assets from looming threats.

Chapter 8. In-depth Analysis: Technical Problems and Their Solutions

As we explore the landscape of MFA, one of the most formidable roadblocks that repeatedly presents itself is its technical challenges. However, daunting as they may seem, these challenges offer opportunities for improvement when confronted with detailed knowledge and effective solution strategies.

8.1. Network Latency

Internet connectivity is a critical component of MFA. A poor-quality or inconsistent connection can slow down the authentication process, potentially causing timeout errors and resulting in a failed authentication. This issue primarily impacts industries and regions that do not have consistent access to high-quality internet.

Solution: One possible mitigation strategy is offline MFA. Authentication apps like Google Authenticator, which use Time-Based One-Time Passwords (TOTP), can function without consistent internet connectivity, offering a viable solution to those affected by network latency issues.

8.2. Inadequate User Education

The effectiveness of MFA ultimately rests on the user. If they are not adequately trained or informed about the importance and the process of MFA, they are more likely to choose weak forms of authentication or bypass it entirely.

Solution: Regular, targeted user education programs can mitigate this issue. Organizations should hold frequent cybersecurity training sessions that focus not only on the basics of MFA but also elaborate on the latest threats and security trends.

8.3. Device Loss

Device loss or theft remains a significant issue when using methods of authentication that require possession of that particular device, such as SMS-based or app-based OTPs.

Solution: A potential solution is the use of biometric identifiers as an authentication factor. Although not perfect, biometrics lessen the risks associated with device loss or theft as they use intrinsic properties of the user, such as fingerprints or facial recognition.

8.4. Incidences of MFA Bypass

In a number of cases, attackers have been successful in bypassing MFA, raising concerns about its capacity to protect an individual's data. This often involves advanced phishing techniques that trick the user into revealing their credentials and their second factor.

Solution: Security measures such as anti-phishing policies, advanced threat protection (ATP), and continual user education can address this problem. Management of service providers, API security, and botnet detection should also be strengthened to mitigate the bypass risk.

8.5. Problems with Biometric Authentication

One major challenge with biometric authentication is inaccurate recognition. For instance, fingerprint scanners could fail to accurately recognize the fingerprint if the finger is wet or dirty.

Solution: Multi-modal biometric authentication can be a solution. This involves combining two or more biometric identifiers, such as fingerprint and face recognition. This can help with increasing the accuracy of biometric authentication and reducing instances of false positives and negatives.

8.6. Implementation Challenges for Small and Medium-Sized Enterprises (SMEs)

The cost and technical expertise required to implement MFA are significant deterrents for SMEs, leaving them more vulnerable to security breaches.

Solution: The usage of cloud-based MFA services can be beneficial for SMEs. These services often offer a more cost-effective and simpler form of MFA, reducing the resources required for implementation.

Looking beyond these technical challenges, the complexities of reliable and efficient MFA implementation persist. However, there's an increasing array of solutions responding to these challenges, delivered by a cybersecurity industry that's driven to innovate as threats evolve.

Please note that all the advice offered here should be tailored to your unique context and circumstances. After all, every organization's cybersecurity needs are different, necessitating a carefully customized approach to their MFA system. Forethought in this process can save a lot of time, resources, and potential hardship in the future.

Chapter 9. Practical Strategies for MFA Error Resolution

Understanding the realities of Multi-Factor Authentication (MFA) error resolution necessitates a hands-on approach to troubleshooting and problem-solving. This in-depth exploration uncovers key practical strategies to effectively navigate the churning waters of MFA error resolution.

9.1. Identification of Common MFA Errors

To begin with, let's familiarize ourselves with the most usual MFA errors organizations may encounter:

1. MFA Type Incompatibility: Occurs when a user's chosen MFA method is not compatible with the supporting infrastructure.

2. Incorrect MFA Enforcement: Happens when the MFA setting doesn't correctly enforce authentication rules.

3. User Lockout: Occurs when a user gets locked out of their account due to MFA error.

4. Time Synchronization: Finds grounds when the timing of the MFA server and user's device is not synchronized, leading to failure in generating the correct codes.

5. Network Connectivity: Issues may arise when either the user or the MFA server has poor network connectivity.

Having identified the common MFA errors, we dive into practical strategies to mitigate them.

9.2. Troubleshooting MFA Type Incompatibility

If an MFA type such as fingerprint scanning or smart card is found to be incompatible with the existing infrastructure, here are the suits-all strategies:

1. Upgrade: Tally your authentication technology with the supporting infrastructure, making necessary system upgrades to facilitate the adoption of the chosen MFA technology.

2. Migration: Where upgrading is not feasible, shift to a compatible MFA type that aligns with the system currently in place.

9.3. Resolving Incorrect MFA Enforcement

Incorrect MFA enforcement can be rectified by employing following strategies:

1. Error Audit: Identify through system logs where the enforcement of MFA rules is falling apart.

2. Policy Adjustment: After the issue is identified, correct the discrepancy by adjusting the MFA policy appropriately.

9.4. Mitigating User Lockout

User lockout can cause significant disruption and should be addressed immediately:

1. Access Recovery: Administrate the ability to recover the original access, preferably through an additional license granted to a trustable party within the organization.

2. Bypass Code: Generate a temporary bypass code that allows the user to circumvent MFA temporarily, ideally with defined expiry time.

9.5. Correcting Time Synchronization Errors

Time synchronization between servers and user devices is essential for successful MFA application:

1. Time Protocol: Use an automatic time-updating protocol, such as Network Time Protocol (NTP), to synchronize time across devices.

2. Manual Correction: Enable the option for users to manually adjust their device's time when necessary.

9.6. Addressing Network Connectivity

Connectivity problems can significantly hinder successful MFA implementation:

1. Redundant Paths: Implement a network design with redundant paths to ensure uninterrupted server availability.

2. Offline Access: Consider an MFA method that can work offline, like biometrics or hardware tokens.

9.7. Preventive Measures and Continuous Improvement

While resolving MFA errors is absolutely essential, the ultimate goal should be their prevention and continuous improvement of MFA processes:

1. Proactive Monitoring: Regularly scan for failures or vulnerabilities.

2. User Education: Regularly conduct training programs to educate users on how to use MFA correctly.

3. Incident Mapping: Develop a clear sequence of steps that need to be taken in case of potential MFA failures.

4. Regular Review: Policy and practices should be reviewed and updated regularly to cope with evolving threats.

By understanding the strategies to resolve MFA errors discussed in this section, organizations can become equipped to make more informed decisions regarding MFA implementation and troubleshoot issues as they arise. Remember, the goal is always to be one step ahead of threats, while never forsaking the user experience. After all, secure and content users are the backbone of a thriving digital organization.

Chapter 10. The Future of Multi-Factor Authentication

As we look to the horizon of digital security practices, Multi-Factor Authentication (MFA) stands as a crucial beacon owing to its extensive capability to safeguard data. Nevertheless, following the spiral of emerging technologies, MFA will inevitably transform to accommodate the evolving digital landscape, raising valid questions about its future directions and adaptations.

10.1. Predicted Changes in MFA Technologies

The first aspect to consider in assessing the future of MFA is the technological revolution and its influence. The advent of emerging technologies such as artificial intelligence (AI), machine learning (ML), blockchain, and quantum computing has created a plethora of opportunities for advancing MFA.

AI and ML have the potential to turn the tables on authentication methods. By learning user behavior and habits, these technologies can build accurate models of what defines 'normal' user behavior, hence enhancing the accuracy of anomaly detection. This adoption of behavioral biometric verification is expected to boost MFA's efficiency and reliability significantly.

On the other hand, quantum computing presents a new layer of challenges as well as opportunities. While on the downside, it could potentially be a threat to current cryptographic methods, it could, conversely, also lead to the development of quantum-resistant cryptography, affirming MFA's prowess in securing data, even from quantum cyber threats.

Blockchain technology also holds expansive potential in MFA, empowering decentralization and ensuring data integrity. This technology can register and secure each authentication element on a distributed ledger, thus enhancing transparency and robustness of the authentication process.

10.2. The Role of User Experience

The user experience (UX) with MFA plays a pivotal role in its widespread adoption, and as such, is expected to evolve significantly in the future. Current MFA methods, while highly secure, sometimes lack in user-friendliness, leading to a reluctance in adoption. Thus, providing a satisfying UX without compromising security stands paramount in shaping the future of MFA.

Trends are already indicating a more seamless and less intrusive MFA experience. Future MFA systems will aim for zero friction, utilizing factors that can be gathered without user input, such as location, biometrics, and behavior. With advancements in machine learning, dynamic and progressive MFA systems could adapt their authentication requirements based on the associated risk of a user's actions.

10.3. The Emergence of Adaptive MFA

Adaptive MFA, an emerging trend in the authentication solutions landscape, promises to revamp security protocols. Capitalizing on contextual and user behavior data, it offers personalized authentication processes based on the risk associated with a session.

For instance, logging in from a recognized IP address during usual working hours may only require single-factor authentication, while accessing sensitive information from a new location may trigger additional authentication layers. Such adaptivity promises a secure yet user-friendly MFA experience, catalyzing widespread adoption.

10.4. Regulatory Influence

The regulatory environment will also be a significant determinant in shaping up the future of MFA. As cyber threats become increasingly sophisticated, governments around the world are ramping up their data privacy regulations.

For example, the General Data Protection Regulation (GDPR) in the European Union, mandates certain types of businesses to implement MFA. Similar regulations are percolating across the globe, necessitating the domain to design solutions around these stipulations to ensure compliance.

10.5. The Future of Biometrics in MFA

Biometrics, which includes fingerprint, facial recognition, voice recognition, and more, are becoming increasingly popular as one of the factors in MFA. The use of biometrics promises advanced security, provided the sensitivity of such personal information is meticulously handled.

Innovations such as vein recognition, heart rhythm identification, and other body-specific biometrics are in the pipeline, significantly enhancing the robustness and conclusivity of identity verification. However, it also throws glaring challenges around data protection regulations and user acceptance, issues that need adequate resolutions before these technologies can fully bloom.

In conclusion, the future of MFA appears to be destined for an era of transformation and advancement. Technological interventions, adaptive solutions, user-centric designs, regulatory adjustments, and advanced biometrics all contribute to reshaping the future MFA landscape. However, alongside these advancements, parallelly evolving cyber threats pose a constant challenge. Therefore, ensuring a far-sighted, all-encompassing approach towards the evolution of MFA is necessary to resiliently safeguard digital identities and data.

Chapter 11. Steps to Enhance MFA Security and User Experience

The increasing prevalence of digital threats has instigated a surge in the adoption of Multi-Factor Authentication (MFA). Businesses, now more than ever, are keen on implementing resilient authentication systems that deter potential compromises. However, strengthening security measures should not mean discounting the user experience (UX). In fact, organizations that achieve a balance between impenetrable security and seamless UX usually witness higher degrees of user compliance and MFA adoption.

11.1. Understanding User Experience in MFA

The debate between fortifying secure access and maintaining optimal end-user experience has always been a fine balancing act. No matter how complex or secure an MFA system is, it's unlikely to succeed if users find it daunting and inconvenient.

To enhance user experience, it's important to consider factors like ease-of-use and simplicity, unobtrusive implementation, and user preference. It's also critical to ensure users understand not just the 'how', but also the 'why' behind MFA. Properly educating users on the importance and advantages of MFA significantly aids in driving adoption.

11.2. Adapting to Contextual MFA

Contextual Multi-Factor Authentication, sometimes referred to as

Adaptive MFA, is an intelligent system that adapts security measures based on a user's behavioral context. It takes into consideration aspects such as geographical location, IP addresses, device type, time of access, and more.

For instance, if a user routinely logs in from a specific device and location, the system recognizes this and allows unimpeded access. However, if suddenly this user tries to access the account from an unknown device or a different location, the system triggers additional authentication requirements.

Such adaptive mechanisms drastically improve user experience. Since security measures are intensified only when the system detects a deviation from the known user patterns, users without anomalous behavior aren't bothered with unnecessary security steps.

11.3. Robustness Against Emerging Threats

In the face of evolving threats, it's crucial for organizations to opt for MFA systems that are future-ready and can withstand even the most sophisticated cyber-attacks.

A reputable MFA solution not only uses the latest algorithms and encryption techniques but also frequently updates its systems to proactively guard against new vulnerabilities. It should be a top priority for organizations to regularly update their MFA systems and educate end-users about security best practices.

11.4. Selecting Appropriate MFA Factors

A user-friendly MFA implementation hinges on the selection of the right MFA factors that align with user behavior and preference.

However, while balancing the user experience, it's equally crucial to maintain the system's robustness against attacks.

The most common factors include:

- Something you know (like a password)
- Something you have (like a token or smartphone)
- Something you are (biometrics)

For better UX, organizations may allow users to select their preferred factors from various options. However, certain situations might demand the implementation of specific factors to maintain the highest level of security, even if they might not be the most convenient ones.

11.5. Streamlining User Registration & Recovery

Signnificant user experience issues arise during the registration process for MFA. Complicated setup processes can discourage user enrollment, hence simplicity is key.

In addition, organizations should streamline the process to recover from a lost or forgotten authentication factor. Readily available recovery methods not only save time but also enhance the user experience. Communication is critical during this process to ensure the user is aware of the next steps, what's happening, and why it's necessary.

11.6. Continuous User Training and Feedback

Continual user education on navigating MFA, its benefits, and updates are instrumental in maintaining a positive user experience. Regular feedback sessions can further dictate improvements in the MFA process and adapt the system to align more closely with user needs and acceptance.

In conclusion, enhancing MFA security while maintaining user experience is a challenging but essential task. By paying attention to user needs, optimizing authentication processes, and ensuring robust security, organizations can navigate this balance, fostering a more secure and user-friendly environment.